DEDICATED:

To the service men and women of our military, with the desire to help and give hope to their children and families, who they leave behind in order to serve this great nation and each of us.

WITH GRATITUDE:

To our families, loved ones, and friends for their encouragement, love, and support. To the many additional counselors associated with the military and other key individuals serving the military, whose contributions and insights were invaluable. And to those military families who, having had many deployment experiences, graciously shared their time, shortcomings, suggestions, understanding, and wisdom. Special thanks to Jan, Sherry, Amanda, Michelle, and Julie.

CREATIVE TEAM:

Concept and Direction: Joel Brandley, MS, MC, LCMHC.
Author and Editor: Jared Brandley.
Illustration and Design: Duke Brandley.

Subject Matter Expert: Lynnette Johnson, LCSW.

Comments and questions can be submitted to us at:
www.militaryfamiliesfortified.com.
Bios and additional copies are also available there.

HURBLE-FLURBLE
★ MILITARY SERIES ★

The stories in the Hurble-Flurble Military Series are adapted from true-life experiences and successes of military families. Our goal is to address the hardships that military families experience through enjoyable stories that are fun and helpful to children and adults.

The Hurble-Flurble is an ageless, caring, wonderfully whimsical character who has grown up in a military family. Over the years, he has developed the wisdom, understanding, and insight that help him connect, comfort, listen, and reach out to adults and children of all ages. His kind, loving, and playful nature allows him to have fun with children and help families find hope and happiness in their everyday lives.

HURBLE-FLURBLE
★ MILITARY SERIES ★

Ben's
TERRIBLE
TANTRUM

The Hurble-Flurble woke one morning,
a big smile on his face,

"I think I'll visit my friend Ben,
who lives up on the Base!"

He walked a bit, went through the gate,
and finally found the street.

He heard a lot of yelling,
so he hurried up his feet!

Ben's mom was in the front yard there,
and she and Ben were *MAD!*

They both were talking *VERY LOUD*,
which made the Hurble sad.

Ben had pulled his sister's hair;
mom sent him to his room.

Ben kicked his bike as he was going,
which made mom's temper **ZOOM!**

"You're grounded 'til your Dad comes home!"

"I DON'T CARE!" he replied.

And then Ben **SLAMMED** the front door hard,
as he stomped off inside.

Ben's mom turned and saw the Hurble,
"I feel I'm going to **BURST!**

Ever since his dad deployed
he's gotten **WORSE** and **WORSE!**"

"I'm sorry," said the Hurble,
"and I know just what you mean!

It seems like just the other day
that I was in that scene!

I don't know if you knew it,
but when I was just a kid,

My dad was in the service too,
and I did what Ben did!"

"We left our home in Hurbleville
and moved onto the Base,

At first I thought that it was cool;
an adventure, a new place!

But when my dad was first deployed,
I missed him quite a lot,

The longer he was far away,
the **ANGRIER** I got!"

"I **KICKED** the walls and yelled at mom...

...she'd ground me more and more,

Until it seemed I'd **NEVER EVER**

walk out our front door!"

"Mom couldn't take a minute more, and so we went to see...

If our friend, the Wise Wabnado,
could help both her and me!"

"She told him what was going on;
he listened close, then said,

'You need to see beyond his actions,
to what is in his head!

EMOTION is what's driving him;
he can't help how he feels,

And how he acts is showing
his frustration's **VERY REAL!**'"

Explain you're sad and lonely too,
when dad is not at home.

It hurts inside when he is gone,
and you feel all alone.'"

"'If **YOU** can talk about your fears,
and how you miss dad, too,

Then **HE** can let his feelings out,
and share them all with you.

And maybe you can hug a bit,
and tell him it's OK,

And both of you can talk some more,
and make it through the day.'"

"My mom took his advice to heart;
it helped us, and we grew.

And if **YOUR** family tries it out,
it might just help you, too!"

"It's worth a try," Ben's mother said.
"Is there more that we can do?"

"Yes, there's lots of ways
to make it easier for you..."

"And though you're sometimes sad and lonely,
do your best to cope.

Keep focused on the future good,
and give your family **HOPE!**

I think I'll head on home today,
but I'll come back again,

To check on you and Ben and see
how you are doing then!"

A few weeks later, the Hurble
went to Ben's and saw, with joy,

A **HAPPY** family playing;
smiling mom, and girl, and boy!

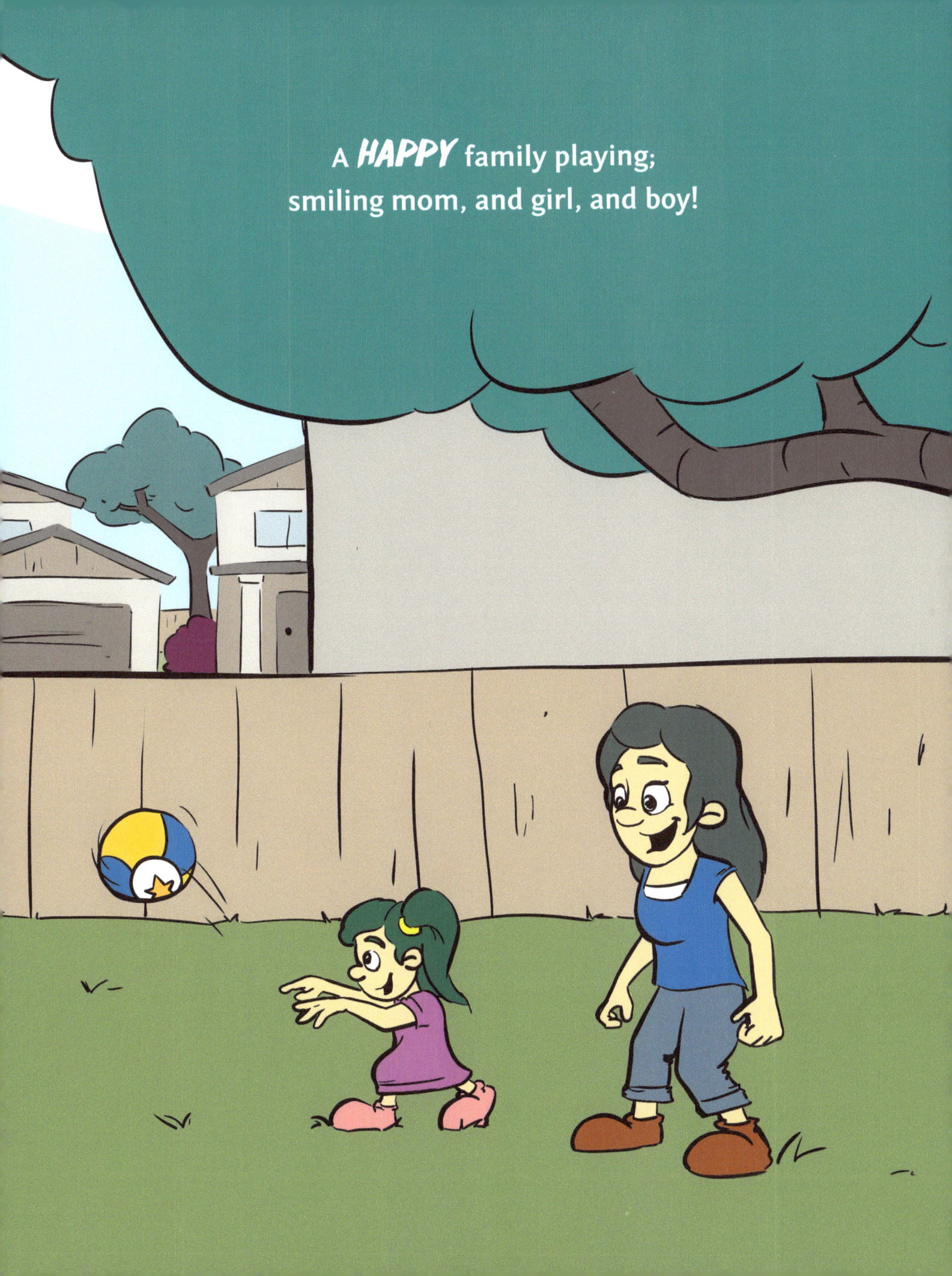

"Hi!" said Ben, "Come have some fun!
We'll laugh and run and play!"

And Ben's mom said, "Your ideas **WORKED!**
We **TALK** more every day!"

"Ben was so surprised to find
that I was lonely, too.

His sister felt that way as well,
and we talked it all right through!

"Hooray!" the Hurble-Flurble grinned.
"Hey, Ben! Toss me that ball!"

They laughed and played together
and were happy, one and all.

"We all are feeling better now,
we know more what to do.

Deployment's not a lot of fun,
but **WE'LL MAKE IT**, thanks to you!"

At last, when it was time to go,
they waved and said, "So long!"

And Ben's mom said, "We'll keep on talking!
TOGETHER we'll be **STRONG!**"

"I'm glad," the Hurble smiled and said,
"Keep trying every day!

It's better sharing how you feel,
and now **YOU'RE ON YOUR WAY!**"

THE END

THIS STORY

As parents, we sometimes focus on our children's actions or behaviors. Out of frustration, we react by adding more and more of the same consequences.

This story suggests we look past their actions to see what is happening inside them. It teaches us that sharing our emotions helps children see that their feelings are normal. By sharing our feelings with them, they learn that they can share their feelings with us.

Children are easily overwhelmed with the emotional chaos growing and bubbling up inside them and they often don't have the words to describe it. Too often, they blame themselves for what is happening in their life, like their dad or mom being gone on a deployment.

As parents, when we help children identify and label their feelings, they can focus on positive action steps to address their emotions. Giving them choices will empower them.

TALKING ABOUT EMOTIONS

The character Ben is a 6-year-old boy. At this age, a child believes that what happens in their world is because of them. They think they are to blame for things which do or do not happen in their life. Here are a few suggestions for helping children, especially at Ben's age:

1) Reduce the number of words you use for feelings. Help them simplify the jumbled-up chaos in their minds by narrowing it down to a few primary emotions; fear, hurt, guilt, shame, or sadness.

2) When a child comes to you distressed, help them identify their feelings clearly and get them to decide which one needs the most attention right then.

3) Once they have identified the most urgent feeling, help them come up with 1 or 2 action steps they can take to address it. For more information on what the 7 primary emotions are and how to address them, go to: www.militaryfamiliesfortified.com.

DEVELOPMENTAL HINTS

Children between the ages of 5-7 are learning to trust (or mistrust) the world around them. They either gain a sense of autonomy doing things for themselves or develop shame and doubt. By Ben's age, they can struggle with guilt or take simple steps to find success. Parents can encourage positive development in several ways:

1) Help them find success by making simple, positive choices. Let them feel they are taking the initiative and doing something constructive to gain control over their difficult situation.

2) Don't blame all their behavior on deployment. A deployment may increase some behaviors, but children Ben's age, as part of their normal developmental growth, are already dealing with:

   a) Increased moodiness, tantrums, crying, and being clingy.

   b) Arguing, fighting with siblings and peers, and falling behind in school.

   c) Having sleep disruptions, nightmares, and wanting to sleep with a sibling or with you.

3) Help them know that sharing their thoughts and feelings is welcome. Encourage them with positive words and actions to address their overwhelmed thinking and feelings. For more developmental hints, go to: www.militaryfamiliesfortified.com.

SELF-ACKNOWLEDGEMENT

1) Give yourself a lot of credit for being willing to support someone that loves you, their family, and their country.

2) Allow yourself to appropriately share some of your thoughts and feelings with your children. It normalizes the bubbling chaos and questions that children are dealing with. Lead by example.

3) Connect with others who are also dealing with a deployed family member.

4) Be willing to seek additional help from professionals as needed and do so before you are overwhelmed and it affects your whole family. Some professionals are listed in the Helping Resources section.

5) Arrange for time for yourself. Having an afternoon or evening to yourself recharges you and allows you to maintain a positive parenting perspective.

For additional fun and creative ideas and information that have worked for other families, go to our website for a free download.

If this story has touched your heart and helped your familiy, please donate and help us create additional stories and resources to fortify our military families.

Visit www.MilitaryFamiliesFortified.com

MILITARY FAMILIES FORTIFIED

HELPFUL RESOURCES

You can seek further help from some of the following resources:

- The Chaplain's office
- Military and Family Life Counselors
- Family Advocacy Program
- Army Community Services
- Airman and Family Readiness Center
- Installation Family Center
- Fleet and Family Services
- Military OneSource
- Your spouse's unit
- Key Spouse organizations
- Behavioral health professionals
- Off-base counselors
- School counselors
- DOD Safe Helpline (safehelpline.org or 1-877-995-5247)

www.ingramcontent.com/pod-product-compliance
Lightning Source LLC
Chambersburg PA
CBHW060813090426
42737CB00002B/55